Classic Student Drinking Games

Ian Ebriated

Crombie Jardine
PUBLISHING LIMITED
Office 2
3 Edgar Buildings
George Street
Bath
BA1 2FJ

www.crombiejardine.com

This edition was first published by
Crombie Jardine Publishing Limited in 2009

ISBN 978-1-906051-39-6

Printed in the UK by CPI William Clowes Beccles NR34 7TL

IMPORTANT WARNING:

DRINKING EXCESS ALCOHOL CAN DAMAGE YOUR HEALTH.

The publisher urges care and caution in the pursuit of any practices related to the activities represented in this book.

This book is intended for use by adults only.

The publisher cannot accept any responsibility for the result of the use or misuse of this book or any loss, injury or damage caused thereby.

Contents

Musical Chairs

Strength rating: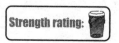

You will need:
- drink
- friends
- chairs
- music

Rules:

Arrange the chairs in a circle facing outwards, making sure there is one chair less than the number of players.

One person acts as the DJ and plays some music while the players walk around the chairs with their drinks in their hands.

When the music stops they must all try to sit down.

Whoever fails to get a seat must have some of their drink, and is out of the game.

Whoever spills their drink in the scramble must also drink, but they continue in the game.

Remove a chair and repeat the game, losing one person and one chair in each round until there is an eventual winner.

The Magic Roundabout

You will need:
- drink
- friends
- a pack of cards

Rules:

Spread the cards out in a circle, to form the 'roundabout'.

One player picks a card. Then the person next to them picks a card.

If the cards are of the same suit, add up the values of the two cards and the two people have to take that number of gulps of their drink.

If they aren't of the same suit then the first person puts their card in a discard pile and the next person draws a card.

If it matches the second person's suit then they drink a number of gulps equal to the combined value of the two cards.

If you get three cards of the same suit in a row, or even four, add up to total value and drink that number.

Mallet's Mallet

Strength rating:

You will need:
- drink
- friends
- a pack of cards

Rules:
Each player has their own drink. Discard all cards from 2 to 9 (inclusive). Place a full glass of drink in the middle of the table, and spread the 20 remaining cards face down, around the glass. Take it in turns to draw a card, performing the following actions according to the card drawn:

10
'Mallet's Mallet'. Play a quick round of word association (one word each, must be related to the previous word, hesitation or irrelevance is punished by drinking).

Jack
Everyone drinks.

Queen
Everyone drinks.

King
That player nominates one person to drink.

Ace
Nothing happens when the first three Aces are drawn, but whoever draws the final Ace must drink the entire glass in the centre of the table.

Pass the Buck

 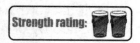
You will need:

- drink
- friends
- a coin

Rules:

This game is similar to pass the parcel, but requires much less preparation.

Everyone sits in a circle except for the DJ, who is responsible for playing and stopping the music.

Players must pass a coin around the circle. Whoever is holding the coin when the music stops must have a drink. If it is in the hands of two people, mid-exchange, they must both drink.

Eye-Spy

 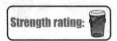

You will need:
- drink
- friends

Rules:
Pick someone to go first, who then thinks of an object within everyone's view. They tell them the letter it begins with, e.g. 'D' if they choose a door, and each person in turn has three chances to guess the object.

If they fail, they must have some of their drink and the next person has three guesses. Whoever guesses correctly must choose the next object.

Straw Football

You will need:
- drink
- friends
- some drinking straws
- a ping-pong ball

Rules:
Everyone sits around the table, with a drinking straw each. The ball is placed in the middle of the table, and each player attempts to blow the ball off the table, keeping it away from themselves. When the ball flies off the table, the person sitting closest to its point of exit must have some of their drink.

Restricted Words

 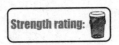
You will need:
- drink
- friends

Rules:

Hold a conversation without using the following words:

The
A
You
Yes
No

Whenever someone uses any of these words they must have a drink.

The Peanut Race

 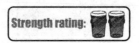
You will need:
- drink
- friends
- a bag of salted peanuts

Rules:

The idea is for each player to drop a peanut into their own full glass at exactly the same time when someone shouts 'Drop!' The peanut will sink to the bottom, then rise up again.

The player whose peanut comes to the surface last is the loser, and must drink their entire glass. The loser's glass is then refilled and another round is played. After a round each player must retrieve the peanut from their glass, eat it, and choose a new one.

Bottles

 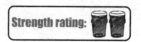

You will need:
- drink
- friends

Rules:
'Bottles' is played in a circle. Someone starts with the number one, and the counting continues in a clockwise direction.

When a number is reached that is a multiple of six, that player must say 'six bottles'. When a number is reached that is a multiple of seven, that player must say 'seven bottles'.

If they forget to say '. . . bottles' they must have some of their drink.

When the counting reaches 100 it goes backwards, and anyone who says the wrong number or forgets to say '. . . bottles' must have a drink.

It's easy counting up, but counting down whilst remembering the 6 and 7 times tables will challenge most people.

Dominoes

 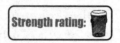
You will need:

- drink
- a box of Dominoes
- a partner

Rules:

This game is a simple as falling off a sofa: if you know how to play Dominoes, and if you know how to drink, you'll have no problem.

Play a standard game of Dominoes, according to the proper rules. But each time one player plays a Domino, the other player must take a gulp of their drink. And that's it!

Taps

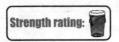

Strength rating:

You will need:
- drink
- friends
- a coin for each player

Rules:

A player taps their coin on the table once to begin play to the right. The person to their right then taps their coin once to maintain that direction, or twice to reverse directions. When a player screws up (tapping out of turn or not tapping soon enough) they must have a drink.

The Personality Game

You will need:
- drink
- friends

Rules:
Sit around a table. The first person turns to the person on their right and says the name of a famous person.

The next person has to think of a personality whose name begins with the first letter of the previous famous person's surname, e.g. if the first celebrity named is Bill *C*linton, the next one could be *C*arrie

Fisher, and the next could be *Fred Astaire*, and so on.

This continues around the table and will only reverse directions if someone says a name where the first letter of the first name and the first letter of the surname are the same, such as *Boris Becker*.

The most important rule is that you must play this game without pausing. If you do pause you have to 'Drink While You Think!' – continuous drinking until you think of a person.

Buzz

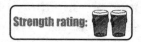

Strength rating:

You will need:
- drink
- friends

Rules:

Sit in a circle.

The first person says 'one', the next person says 'two' and so on.

However when someone reaches a number divisible by six they must say 'buzz'.

If the player doesn't say 'buzz', hesitates, or gets their number wrong, they must down a previously agreed upon quantity of their drink.

The word 'buzz' changes the direction and to make things harder add in 11 and say 'bizz' for numbers divisible by 11, keeping 'buzz' for numbers divisible by 6. The direction of play changes for each 'buzz' or 'bizz'.

Whizz, Bounce, Boing

Strength rating:

This game requires a degree of mental agility – so play it at the start of an evening; you won't be able to by the time you get to the end!

You will need:
- drink
- friends

Rules:
Everyone sits around a table. There are only three words that can be spoken: Whizz, Bounce, Boing. Someone starts by saying one of the words.

Whizz
The imaginary ball passes to the next player.

Bounce
The ball skips the next the player and goes to the following player.

Boing
The ball hits the wall and reverses direction.

If you make a mistake you have to drink until the others tell you to stop.

Who Am I?

You will need:

- drink
- friends
- a pen and paper
- some sticky tape

Rules:

One player writes down the name of a famous person on a piece of paper and sticks it to the forehead of another player. Everyone can see the name on the paper except the person on whose forehead it is stuck. This person must find out who they are by asking questions to each player in turn. Only 'yes' or 'no' may be given as answers. For every 'no' given the person asking the questions must have some of their drink.

The James Bond Game

You will need:
- drink
- friends
- a James Bond film

Rules:
You must have a drink whenever one of the following occurs:

- Someone says 'James'

- Someone says 'Bond'

- Bond makes a cheesy comment to Moneypenny

- Bond gets a new gadget
- Bond wears a dinner suit
- Bond seduces a woman
- Someone attempts to kill Bond
- Bond gets told off by M or Q
- Someone speaks with a Russian accent
- A Bond girl wears a bikini
- Bond drinks a vodka martini
- Felix appears
- There is a car chase
- Bond makes a cheesy pun
- Something explodes
- Bond breaks a new gadget
- The Bond theme is played

Sentence

 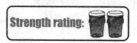
You will need:

- drink
- friends

Rules:

Someone starts with a word, any word. The next person has to say a word that could make a sentence with the word that has just been said, and so on.

The game goes on until someone says a word that doesn't make sense, or until someone hesitates, or until they laugh so much that they can't talk. This person then has to have a drink and the game continues.

The sentences constructed when this game is played can become absolutely bizarre, especially if some of the players are lateral thinkers, but as long as the sentence makes grammatical sense it will count.

Rhyme Without Reason

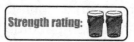

Strength rating:

You will need:
- drink
- friends

Rules:

Someone starts with a random word. The person next to them has to say a word that rhymes with this. When someone repeats a word or they can't think of a rhyme, they must have some of their drink. It is their turn to start again with a new word.

Polysyllabic words are usually difficult to rhyme with, so when it's your turn to think of a word, choose a long one!

Drink-Tac-Toe

 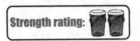

You will need:
- drink
- a partner
- pen and paper

Rules:
This is basically noughts and crosses, or tic-tac-toe, except played with drinking penalties.

The loser of each game must have some of their drink. If they lose three games in a row they must down an entire glass of their drink.

Party Snap

 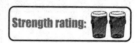
You will need:
- drink
- friends
- a pack of cards

Rules:
The more players, the better. Nominate one person to be the dealer. This role changes with each round because the dealer doesn't get to play that round. The dealer begins by placing cards, face up, in a stack, and calls out the number on each turn.

When two cards of the same number come up in sequence, the first person to bring their hand down onto the top of the pile and shout 'Snap!' gets the top card, and is then allowed to nominate a player to drink a number of gulps of their drink equal to the number of the card.

A round ends when the dealer has no more cards.

Name That Tune

You will need:
- drink
- friends
- a CD player

Rules:
One person is the DJ, and the others take turns to identify songs within their first five seconds. If a song is incorrectly guessed, the player must have some of their drink. A player can choose to attempt identification in less than five seconds, subject to the drinking penalties opposite if they get it wrong.

40

Drinking penalties

A wrong guess at 4 seconds

penalty:

2 gulps

A wrong guess at 3 seconds

penalty:

3 gulps

A wrong guess at 2 seconds

penalty:

4 gulps

A wrong guess at 1 second

penalty:

the entire drink

Just A Minute

You will need:
- drink
- friends
- a watch

Rules:
The object of the game is to talk for 60 seconds on a subject without repetition, hesitation or deviation.

One player acts as Judge, with responsibility for nominating a subject and keeping time. Another player starts talking about the subject.

If they hesitate, deviate or repeat themself another player can interrupt.

If the interruption is considered valid by the judge, a drinking penalty is handed out to the initial speaker, and the person who interrupted gets to continue talking on the subject for the remainder of the minute.

Each change of speaker results in a drinking penalty for the outgoing speaker.

Whoever is speaking when the minute is up gets to nominate a person to drink, and becomes the judge in the next game.

Fuzzy Duck

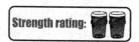

Strength rating:

You will need:
- drink
- friends

Rules:
Sit in a circle. The first person nominated turns to their left and says, 'Fuzzy Duck'. The next person turns to their left and does the same.

This continues until somebody turns to the person who's just said 'Fuzzy Duck' to them, and says 'Duzzy?'

The question 'Duzzy?' can only be asked twice by the same person per round. The question changes the direction and the phrase changes to 'Ducky Fuzz'.

Anyone can reverse the direction by saying 'Duzzy?'

The idea is to go round as fast as you can.

Stalling or getting it wrong means you have to have a drink.

It's probably best not to play this one within earshot of your mother-in-law/local priest/young children; the game can result in some very rude words being thrown about!

Look-Out!

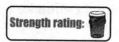

Strength rating:

You will need:
- drink
- friends

Rules:
Sit where you can see people walking by, preferably outdoors. Each person chooses an item of clothing/accessories from the list opposite.

Whenever someone walks past wearing or carrying your item, you take a gulp of your drink. As a variation, types of car or colours of clothing can be used.

List of items:

> **Hat**
> **Briefcase**
> **Umbrella**
> **Shopping bag**
> **Coat**
> **Walking stick**
> **High heels**
> **Wig**
> **Glasses**
> **Dress**

Slap, Clap, Click

Strength rating:

You will need:
- drink
- friends

Rules:
This is one of the hardest games to play...
those without a sense of rhythm will be
in trouble!

Before starting the game a category has
to be decided. Players sit in a circle or
around a table and begin the game by
slapping their thighs with both hands,
then clapping their hands together and

finally clicking their fingers twice. This routine should build up into a steady 4-beat rhythm.

Whilst the players are doing this they have to take turns to call out a word belonging to the category decided, keeping strictly to the rhythm.

If a player fails to think of a word when the beat gets to them, they must have a drink.

If anyone loses rhythm or says a word that doesn't fit the category, they must have a drink.

One Big Chicken

 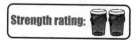

You will need:
- drink
- 8 people

Rules:
Play the game person by person. Each person takes a phrase but the sixth person has to say the sixth phrase as well as repeat the other five phrases. If they get the phrases wrong they have to gulp their drink to the number of phrases they missed and then start with the first phrase again. This carries on until all eight phrases are said without making a single mistake.

Phrases:

- Big chicken

- Sweet ducks

- Furry running rabbits

- Large ladies, sitting, sipping cider, and smoking cigarettes

- Sheets slit by Sam the sheet slitter

- Saucy Siamese sailors sailing the seven seas

- Echoing egoists echoing egotistical ecstasies

- Fig pluckers plucking figs, I'm not a fig plucker or a fig plucker's son but I'll pluck figs until the fig plucking's done!

Joker

You will need:
- drink
- friends
- a pack of cards

Rules:

Everyone sits round in a circle. Place a glass of drink in the middle. Put the pack of cards, Jokers included, in the middle, face down. Someone goes first, taking a card from the top of the pack.

What card they have is indicative of what they have to do:

Ace	=	The player with the card can pick anyone they like to drink
King	=	Everybody has a drink
Queen	=	All women have a drink
Jack	=	All men have a drink
10	=	The 2nd person to the right of that player has to drink
9	=	The 2nd person to the left of that player has to drink
8	=	Everyone has to drink
7	=	The person to the immediate left of that player has a drink
6	=	The person to the immediate right of that player has a drink
5	=	Change direction (i.e., from clockwise to counter-clockwise)
4-2	=	The person choosing takes the number of gulps of their drink on that card

If somebody picks up a Joker then they must either drink the entire glass in the middle, or perform a dare instead.

Matchbox Game

You will need:
- drink
- friends
- a matchbox

Rules:
Each player takes it in turn to throw a matchbox. According to how it lands they must drink the amounts listed opposite.

Face up
1 finger measurement
of their drink

Face down
2 fingers measurement
of their drink

On its side
3 fingers measurement
of their drink

On its end
4 fingers measurement
of their drink

Kings and Blood

You will need:
- drink
- friends
- a pack of cards

Rules:

Shuffle a pack of cards, then spread them out on a table, face down.

Put an empty glass in the middle of the table.

Go around the table drawing the cards, one at a time.

If you draw a red card, have a drink.

If you draw a black card, don't drink.

Whenever you draw one of the Kings, pour some drink into the glass in the centre of the table (the quantity is up to the player).

Whoever draws the final (fourth) King, must drink the centre glass.

The Orange Game

Strength rating:

You will need:
- drink
- friends
- an orange

Rules:

All players stand in a line, and the first one places the orange under their chin. Each player must pass the orange along the line from person to person without using their hands.

Whenever the orange is dropped, the player(s) responsible must have a drink.

Number 99

You will need:
- drink
- friends
- a pack of cards

Rules:
Deal four cards to each player, then turn over the top card and place it in the centre. The object is for each person in turn to place a card in the centre, forming a pile, until the value of that pile is 99. Players must try to calculate and remember the total value of the pile as it grows, for whoever causes the pile to reach 99 or more must have some of their drink.

Once 99 has been reached or exceeded re-shuffle and deal again. After the cards have been played, just take more from the stack. When they run out, re-shuffle the original cards.

Special cards:

Queen: placing a Queen down when the pile approaches 99 puts the drinking responsibility on the person to your left instead of you.

Five: can be used to abdicate from drinking responsibilities.

Ten: when the value of the pile is in the 90s, placing a 10 lowers the value of pile by 10, rather than increasing it.

Socials:

Whenever the total equals a number ending in 9, everyone must have a drink.

Special socials:

Whenever the total equals 69, everyone must have a drink from their neighbour's glass.

The Word Association Game

You will need:
- drink
- friends

Rules:
Someone starts off by saying a word and points at somebody else.

This person has to say a word which is related to the one just said, whilst pointing at someone else and so on.

Names are not allowed.

If someone hesitates, deviates or repeats then they must have some of their drink.

If at any time you think the word association has got a little hard to follow or is simply ridiculous, you can challenge a person.

If they can explain their association, then you must have a drink. If not, then they must do so.

Guess the Note

 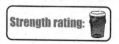
You will need:
- bottles of drink
- friends
- a piano

Rules:
One player takes a seat at the instrument. The other players drink unspecified amounts from their bottles.

The first player blows a note on their bottle, as if playing a flute.

The person at the instrument has three tries to repeat the note with the instrument.

If repeated correctly, the first player has a drink.

If the person can't match the note, they must take three gulps of their drink and pass their turn.

Countdown

 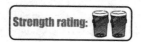
You will need:
- drink
- friends
- a watch with a second hand

Rules:
Each player chooses a number, from 1 to 12.

When the second hand goes past a player's number, they have a drink.

Any player who misses their cue, must drink double during the next minute.

I Went To Market . . .

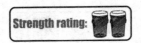

Strength rating:

You will need:
- drink
- friends

Rules:
The first person says, 'I went to market and I bought . . .' and adds the name of an object. The second person has to repeat the entire phrase, adding a second object. The third person repeats everything and adds a third object, and so on. As the list gets longer the chances of making a mistake increase. All mistakes are punishable by drinking.

The Dictator Game

You will need:
- drink
- friends
- a pack of cards

Rules:
Each player takes a card. The player with the highest card is the dictator. The dictator then announces some card-based conditions and deals out up to five cards per player. For every card a player has that meets the announced conditions, they have a drink. The dictator is also dealt a hand of cards, except nominating, rather than taking, a

drink. After each round, the dictatorship passes to the left.

Example conditions: all even cards, all spades, all Aces, etc...

The dictator can, of course, change the rules to whatever they want while they remain in power.

Pyramid Power

You will need:
- drink
- friends
- a pack of cards

Rules:
Build a flat pyramid of cards by placing seven cards face down in a row as the base and building up layers on the table next to it until there is one card as the top.

Jokers aside, distribute the other cards among the players. The dealer turns over the first card at the base of the pyramid and calls out the card value.

Anyone who claims to have a card of the same value nominates a person to have a drink. That person may either drink or call people's bluff by saying 'pyramid power'.

If the first person has the card after all, they show the card and the victim drinks two gulps of their drink. If they don't have it, they drink two gulps themselves.

Once a row of the pyramid is completed, the first card on the next row is drawn, and every card now has the same value penalty as its row, i.e. 2 gulps for this row, 3 for the next row, etc.

Each person with a card on the second row can nominate someone to drink two gulps, on the third row three gulps, all the way up to the seventh row.

All 'pyramid power' calls double the value of the row, of course, making them risky propositions as time goes on.

At the seventh row, if people are taking honest drinks, a 'pyramid power' call should result in the consumption of a full glass.

Chess

 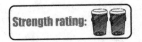

You will need:
- drink
- 2 people
- a chess set

Rules:
The board game is played as usual. Whenever you take an opponent's piece, they must have a drink.

Pawn = 1 gulp
Other pieces = 2 gulps
Queen = 3 gulps
Checkmate = 4 gulps

Kipper Racing

 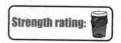

You will need:
- drink
- friends
- newspaper
- a pair of scissors
- some magazines

Rules:

Cut the shape of a kipper from the newspaper for each player.

Place the 'kippers' on the floor in a row.

Each player stands behind their own kipper, and must flap it to the finish line using a magazine.

The last one to get their kipper to the finish line in each game must have some of their drink.

My Hat It Has Three Corners

Strength rating: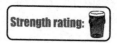

You will need:
- drink
- friends

Rules:

Sit in a circle. One person starts by singing:

> 'My hat it has three corners,
> Three corners has my hat,
> And had it not three corners,
> It would not be my hat.'

Each person around the table follows suit.

When it returns to the first person they remove the word 'hat', replace it with the action of pointing at their head, and everyone else repeats this.

The game continues removing 'three' and replacing it with three fingers, and then removing 'corners' and replacing it with the action of turning a corner in a racing car (accompanied by the noise) respectively.

If you make a mistake you must have a drink.

Play Your Cards Wrong

Strength rating: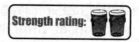

You will need:
- drink
- friends
- a pack of cards

Rules:
Deal a card to a player. That player has to guess whether the next card will be higher or lower.

If the guess is incorrect, the player must have a drink. If the guess was right, they get another go.

If they survive for at least three cards they may choose to continue for another three cards or pass to the next player.

When a player guesses wrongly, they must take a gulp of their drink for each card showing, therefore the idea is to build up as many cards as possible before passing it on to the next player.

If the next card is the same as the current card, this counts as a correct guess.

Coin Football

 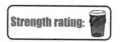
You will need:
- drink
- friends
- 3 coins

Rules:

Two players at a time sit at either end of a wooden table.

One player uses the fingers of their left hand to create a 'goal', while the other player uses one finger to shove the three coins across part of the table towards the goal.

They must then select one coin, and try to shove it between the two others, and again shove a coin through the two others until they get a shot at the goal with one of the coins.

If they score, the other player must have some of their drink.

If they are unable to flick a coin between the other two, play swaps to the other person who puts the three coins together and launches a counter attack.

The loser of each goal must have a drink. If more than two players are present, the winner stays in their seat while someone replaces the loser in each game.

Bluffer!

You will need:
- drink
- up to 6 people
- a pack of cards

Rules:

The object of this game is to get rid of all your cards.

Sit in a circle, deal the cards evenly, and take it in turns to lay face down your Aces, then your twos, etc.

If a player doesn't have any of that sort of card, they must bluff.

If someone thinks they are lying, they say 'Bluffer!'

If that person is right, the bluffer takes a number of gulps of their drink proportional to the number of cards in the stack.

If someone is wrongly accused of bluffing, the accuser must drink the prescribed amount.

Whenever someone has drunk the number of gulps equating to the number of cards in the stack, they must then pick up all the cards in that stack and add them to their own.

The winner is the first to run out of cards.

The Questions Game

Strength rating:

You will need:
- drink
- friends

Rules:
Hold a conversation using only questions. If a player forgets to answer using a question, they must have some of their drink.

Initials

You will need:
- drink
- friends

Rules:

The game starts by one player asking a question to the group, such as 'Who is your favourite pop star?' Each player in turn has to give an answer that corresponds to their initials, i.e. Ricky Smith might reply Rod Stewart, Tessa Thompson might reply Tina Turner... Other categories could include favourite sports personalities or food.

If a person hesitates or can't think of an answer they have to have a drink.

Entwined

You will need:

- drink
- 3-6 friends
- a pack of cards

Rules:

Jokers aside, deal the cards clockwise, face down. Each player must keep their hand out of sight of the other players. The player to the left of the dealer starts by laying down one of their cards, face up. Going clockwise, the other players in turn must each lay down a card of the same face value.

When the play gets to someone who does not have a card of the same face value, that player becomes 'entwined' and must have a drink. The next player may then play any card. If the 'entwined' player doesn't have that card either, they remain entwined, and must have another drink. Play then shifts back to the player to the right of the entwined player. This person then plays any card. This goes back and forth until the 'entwined' player gets released by playing the same face value card as one of the adjacent players.

Play continues until a player plays their last card. Once this happens, the rest of the players must count their remaining cards and take that number of gulps of their drink.

The Motor Racing Game

Strength rating:

You will need:
- drink
- friends
- a television

Rules:
Sit and watch motor racing on the television, drinking according to the formula opposite.

One car crashes or breaks down
= 1 gulp

Two cars collide
= 2 gulps

A pitstop
= 1 gulp

A problem at the pitstop
= 3 gulps

Animal, Vegetable or Mineral . . .

Strength rating:

You will need:
- drink
- friends

Rules:
Take it in turns to think of an object that fits one of the animal, vegetable or mineral categories. The other players have three questions each, to which the person being questioned must answer 'yes' or 'no'. The first general question, which doesn't count, should always be, 'Are you animal, vegetable or mineral?'

If a player fails to guess correctly within three questions they must have a drink and the questioning moves to the next person.

If a player's three questions are all answered 'yes', but without leading to a final identification, that player may continue to ask questions until they receive a 'no' or until they correctly identify the animal, vegetable or mineral.

Riverboat

You will need:
- drink
- at least 12 people
- 2 packs of cards

Rules:

Everyone sits in a circle. One player is nominated the dealer as well as a player. The dealer hands out four cards to everyone, to be kept in front of each player, face up.

The dealer then starts the 'riverboat' by turning over the first card on the deck, and each player with the same card in front of him/her (suit doesn't matter), must have a drink. If the person has more than one of the same card, they must have a drink for each card.

The dealer then turns over the next card. Again, each player with the same card must take a drinking penalty, except this time it is two times the agreed amount per card. The next deal is three times, and the last is four times.

After the fourth card, the dealer sends the 'riverboat' back in the opposite direction by dealing the next card on top of the fourth card dealt.

Players with matching cards now give four drinking penalties away in any combination; four to one player, or maybe one penalty to four different players. The same situation applies if the player has more than one of the same card; the player gives penalties for each card.

The dealer continues cruising back on the riverboat by dealing the next card on top of the third card dealt. This time players nominate three penalties for each matching card.

The next deal is a nomination of two penalties, and the last deal is a nomination of one penalty. After all the cards are dealt, simply shuffle and deal again.

Play continues until everyone has had enough!

The Missing Letter

 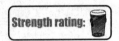

You will need:
- drink
- friends

Rules:
Nominate a letter of the alphabet to be banned from the conversation.

Any letter may replace it.

If a person utters the banned letter by mistake, they must have a drink.

The Flicks

You will need:

- drink
- friends
- a coin each
- an empty glass

Rules:

The object of this game is not to win or lose, merely to keep in the game. Essentially, all you have to do is to flick a coin on its flat side into the empty glass.

Each player takes a turn at doing this, and when anyone succeeds they can nominate another person to take a gulp of their drink. They must continue to take flicks of the coin until they miss. When a player misses, they can have another attempt if they want, but a second failure is punished by drinking themselves.

When a player has scored three consecutive successful shots, they can nominate every other player to drink two times the agreed amount each.

Queens

Strength rating:

You will need:
- drink
- friends
- a pack of cards

Rules:
Jokers aside, shuffle the cards, then spread them out on the table so that any can be chosen.

Take it in turns to pick a card at random, then perform the duties opposite according to the cards selected.

Ace	=	Choose any player to drink
King	=	All players drink
Queen	=	Women drink
Jack	=	Men drink
10	=	2nd person to right of chooser must drink
9	=	2nd person to left of chooser drinks
8	=	All players drink
7	=	Person to right of chooser drinks
6	=	Person to left of chooser drinks
5	=	Change direction of play
4 to 2	=	Chooser must take that number of gulps of their drink

Strength rating:

You will need:

- drink
- friends
- a beer mat

Rules:

This is the simplest game *on the planet*, and therefore highly recommended for those who feel they are *off it*.

Take a beer mat, and flip it into the air.

If it lands face up, nominate someone to have some of their drink.

If it lands face down, you have to drink.

Each person takes it in turns to flip the mat, with a 50-50 chance of having to take a drink themselves or nominate someone else!

The game works best if people conspire to nominate just one person to have a drink whenever they win.

The Blow Off Game

You will need:
- drink
- friends
- a pack of cards
- an empty bottle

Rules:
First, place the cards on the empty bottle. Each player blows cards off the deck on the bottle in turn.

If a player spots an Ace among the cards that have been blown off, that player has to have a drink. It is then their turn to 'blow off'.

If two Aces are visible that person has to drink two times the agreed amount.

The player who blows the last card off the bottle has to drink one glass of their drink.

Pick a Straw

You will need:
- drink
- friends
- a straw (or blade of grass) for each player

Rules:

Get a plastic straw for each player. Each straw must be the same length.

Cut one straw short and place them all in your fist so that they all look the same length.

Each player must pick a straw. Whoever draws the short straw must have a drink.

For the next round, cut short a second straw so that there will be two losers. In the third round, cut short three, and so on.

Harry

 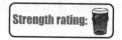

You will need:
- drink
- friends

Rules:

Players need to sit in a circle or around a table. The game starts by one player looking at another player and saying 'Harry?'

The second person must respond by saying 'Yes Harry?' to the first person, who then says 'Tell Harry'. That concludes the first round.

The next stage is for the second person to say 'Harry?' to third member of the group, who must then respond by saying 'Yes Harry?' to the second player and in turn the second player must say 'Yes Harry?' again to the first player.

The first player who started the game again says 'Tell Harry'. Simple really!

If a player slips up or hesitates they must have a drink and they are then known as 'Harry One Spot'.

I Have Never . . .

You will need:
- drink
- friends

Rules:

Sit in a circle.

The first person has to make a true statement such as, 'I have never been to Disneyland.'

If another person has done what the first person hasn't done then the first person has to have a drink.

Every true statement has to begin with 'I have never . . .'

If played correctly, you can discover some real home truths by a process of elimination and as people become more lucid . . . so it's probably best not to play this with your boss!

Card Head

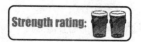

Strength rating:

You will need:
- drink
- friends
- a pack of cards

Rules:
Players sit in a circle.

Decide whether Ace is high or low.

Each player is dealt a card which they have to stick on their forehead without looking at it.

If you can't get the card to stay on your head hold it on with your finger.

You'll be able to see the value of your fellow players' cards but you won't have any idea what your own card is.

The idea is to gamble as to whether you think your own card is higher than that of your friends.

If you take a bet and lose, you must have a drink.

Charades

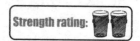

Strength rating:

You will need:
- drink
- friends

Rules:
Take it in turns to mime a book, a song or a film. Other players must guess what is being mimed, but for every incorrect guess they make, they must have a drink. Whoever guesses correctly gets to do the next mime.

Speaker

 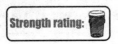

You will need:
- drink
- friends

Rules:

Only one person is the 'speaker'. The speaker begins by saying '1,2,3, DRINK!'

Everybody must take a drink until the speaker feels ready to shout again, '4,5,6, DRINK!' and so on.

This is a great one to play if you lack conversational skills or are at a boring party!

Yes, Prime Minister

Beware of being excessively cruel in this game – as in politics, what goes around, comes around.

You will need:
- drink
- friends
- a pack of cards

Rules:

To start with, everyone draws a card from the pack which is face down. The person who gets the highest card is the Prime Minister. All the other players are mere MPs, bureaucrats etc. The bottom line is that they have to do whatever the PM tells them to do.

The PM now thinks of any (card-based) rule s/he wants (e.g. 'All players with a Royal card must have a drink of . . .'), declares it, and then deals out no more than five cards to each player. Then if anybody has met the conditions (e.g. has a Queen) they have to do as instructed.

For a variation, the Prime Minister could change the forfeits from just taking a drink to performing stupid, embarrassing dares – anything from singing 'Baa, Baa, Black Sheep' in rock 'n' roll style to drinking the number of gulps equal to their age.

This is the whole point of being Prime Minister – to change the rules when it pleases you – it also keeps the game entertaining.

Musical Statues

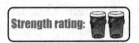

Strength rating:

You will need:
- drink
- friends
- a source of music

Rules:
Nominate one person to act as the DJ.

Players move about normally, with glasses of drink in their hands.

When the music stops, everyone must remain absolutely motionless for 10 seconds.

Anyone who moves noticeably must have a drink.

As the evening wears on, this game will become increasingly difficult as the players become less steady.

Cheers

You will need:
- drink
- friends

Rules:
The game starts when the first person lifts their glass to toast something of their preference, such as 'Cheers to the fine weather!'

Everybody knocks their glasses together and takes two drinks from their glass.

The toasts continue around the table as fast as possible, with each person saying their personal 'Cheers to . . .' and every-body drinking two gulps of their drink each time.

This is a very merry game but it can get quite loud due to the knocking together of glasses and rowdy toasting.

You'll probably find that the volume increases as the toast tally rises!

Sardines

You will need:
- drink
- friends
- somewhere to hide

Rules:
One person takes a full glass of drink and hides with it somewhere in the building or grounds.

The others, each with a glass of drink, must try to find the hider.

When someone finds them, the hider must have a drink from their glass, and the other person now hides with them.

When someone finds them both, they must both drink from their glasses, and all three people now hide.

The last person to find the hidden people must take a number of gulps of their drink equal to the number of people in the hiding place.

International Drinking Rules

 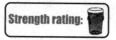

You will need:
- drink
- friends

Rules:

1. No pointing (you can use your elbows to gesture).
2. No swearing.
3. You must drink with the hand that you don't normally use (e.g. your left if you are right-handed) and with your little finger pointing out.

If you break the rules you must have a drink.

This is a copy-cat game, but instead of a 'Simon says . . .' instruction, the players must deduce by observation the action they must copy.

Any player may choose to do an action at any time. For example, someone might decide to put their thumb on their forehead, and everyone has to follow suit.

The last person to catch on has to have a drink.

Happy Shopper

You will need:

- drink
- friends
- pen and paper
- plastic shopping bags
- a watch

Rules:

Make a list of five household items: a piece of toilet paper, a book, a fork, etc., making sure that there will be enough of each to go round (there's no point in putting 'a tin of cat food' down on the list if you only have one!).

Nominate one person to be the referee.

Each of the 'shoppers' must have a plastic shopping bag.

The referee stands at 'base' (e.g. the living room).

When the referee says 'Go!' the players have five minutes in which to find all the items on the list and return home with them to base.

The last person back must down an entire glass of their drink.

Play continues with a new list and referee.

Twenty-One

 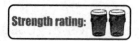
You will need:

- drink
- friends
- a pack of cards

Rules:

The object of the game is to get as close to 21 points in your hand without going over. Aces are 11, all face cards are 10 points, and all other cards are face value.

Deal two cards to each player, one face-down, and one face-up.

The play rotates, like in Pontoon, for additional cards ('twist'). If you think you have a high hand, 18 points or so, you can 'knock', which means everyone else has to take one more card.

After everyone has taken their last card, the hands are laid down and the person with the lowest points total has to have a drink.

If the person who knocked has the lowest points total, that player must also drink an additional penalty for poor play.

If a player gets more than 21, they must have a drink.

If someone has a precise total of 21, everyone else must drink.

The Tackle Game

You will need:
- drink
- friends
- a television

Rules:

Players must divide themselves into two teams, and sit around a television watching a contact sport, such as football or rugby.

Each team on the sofa will identify with one on the television.

Whenever someone from your team makes a tackle, all members of the other team must have a drink.

If a goal or a try is scored, the losing team must drink two times the agreed amount each.

A, B, C

Strength rating:

You will need:
- drink
- friends

Rules:
Sit in a circle.

The players must choose a category, e.g. films.

Play starts with the letter A, with every player having to think of a film (or other word related to the chosen category) beginning with A.

The first person might say 'Armageddon', the next 'All Quiet on the Western Front', with play continuing clockwise.

If a player hestitates or can't think of a word they must have a drink.

Play then resumes with B, then C, until Z is reached, or everyone has had enough, or can no longer speak.

Racing Demon

You will need:
- drink
- friends
- a die
- a selection of old clothes
  (scarf, coat, gloves, trousers, etc.)

Rules:
Sit in a circle.

Place the clothes and a glass of booze in the centre.

Each player takes it in turn to throw the die.

When a player throws a six they must run to the centre of the circle, put on the clothes and drink from the centre glass.

They must continue drinking until another player throws a six and replaces them.

This can be quite a rowdy one – and you'll probably need to top up the centre glass from time to time!

The Telepathy Game

 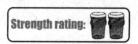

You will need:
- drink
- friends
- a pack of cards

Rules:
Place a pack of cards face down. A player has to guess the colour of the top card: if correct, they get another go; if incorrect they must have a drink and play moves to the next player.

If a player is correct for three cards in a row, everyone else must drink. The player with the best telepathic powers will win by having to drink a lesser penalty.

Guess the Ad

 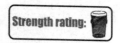

You will need:
- drink
- friends
- a television

Rules:

Put the television on and wait for the adverts to come up. Take it in turns to guess what each advert is for, within five seconds of it starting. If a player gets it wrong they must have a drink. Player two gets the second advert, player three the third, etc.

Usually there will be sufficient adverts for up to five or six people, with opportunities to play coming up every fifteen minutes or so.

135

The Dealer and the Fuzz

You will need:

- drink
- friends
- one playing card per person
- one King and one Ace must be included

Rules:

Players must sit in a circle. The cards are then dealt face down. Everyone takes a quick look at theirs. The person who gets the King is *the fuzz* and the person who gets the Ace is the *dealer*.

The dealer must very discreetly wink at one of the other players, who will eventually say, 'The deal has been made.'

At this time the fuzz identifies themself and tries to guess who the dealer is.

If the fuzz chooses the wrong player they must have a drink.

If they choose wrong again, they must drink the number on the wrongly accused person's card, for example, ten gulps for a ten of clubs.

When the fuzz finally chooses correctly, the dealer has to drink the total number on the remaining cards.

If the dealer wins at the fuzz, the dealer must drink the total number on his/her own card.

After this, the cards are shuffled, re-dealt and the game continues.

Gargle-Gurgle

Strength rating: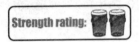

You will need:
- drink
- friends

Rules:
A slightly messier version of Name That Tune. Each player takes it in turns to perform a song for their 'audience'. The catch is that songs cannot be sung - they must be gargled! The other players take turns to identify the song, and an incorrect guess is punished by a drinking penalty. If, after a second gargled rendition, none of the players can guess the tune, the performer must finish an agreed quantity of their drink.

The Genre Game

You will need:
- drink
- friends

Rules:
One person starts the game by calling out a genre, e.g. 'Shakespeare Plays'. The person next to them then has to call out a word that will fit into that category, e.g. 'Hamlet'. When someone repeats a word or they can't think of a new member of that genre, they have to have a drink. It is their turn to start again with a new genre. Example genres could be: Science Fiction Films, Cartoons, Modern Literature, Sequels, Modern Art, etc.

Darts

 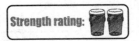
You will need:

- drink
- friends
- a dartboard and darts

Rules:

Each player throws three darts, and must drink according to the following scores:

1 - 20	= 4 gulps
21- 30	= 3 gulps
31- 40	= 2 gulps
41- 50	= 1 gulp
51+	= no penalty

Drinking-Up Time

Strength rating:

You will need:
- drink
- friends
- an egg cup
- a die
- a coin

Rules:
The egg cup, containing the die and the coin, is passed around.

The person throwing the die and the coin does so on behalf of the person to their right, the 'caller'.

This person (the caller) says 'heads' or 'tails'.

If the caller is correct, the person who threw the die and the coin must take the number of gulps shown on the die from their drink (three on the die would mean three gulps of drink).

If the caller is wrong, then they themselves must drink gulps to the number shown on the die.

www.crombiejardine.com